Called To Teach

Dear God, Are You Sure?

---

by

Wendell C Douglas

A Practical Guide For "Called" Teaching

By
Wendell C Douglas

Dedication

To my former students and colleagues, you are the heart and soul of this book. Your enthusiasm for teaching and learning, willingness to take risks, and deep faith have been a constant source of inspiration and joy. Your insights, guidance, goading, and ceaseless humor molded me into the driven, sometimes cynical, and almost delightful person I am today! Your unwavering commitment to excellence inspired me to become a better teacher, learner, administrator, and person.

To my education colleagues, thank you for your support, encouragement, and friendship. Your unwavering commitment to students and passion for teaching has helped create a culture of excellence and a community of learners to which I am proud to belong.

To my former students, thank you for allowing me to join your journey. I am deeply honored to have been part of your life and witnessed your extraordinary growth and transformation. Your curiosity, creativity, and resilience taught me more than I could ever have taught you. May this book inspire you to continue to learn, grow, and serve others with humility, a sense of humor, and life-giving faith.

Finally, I dedicate this work to my wife, whose support, encouragement, and willingness to take up the slack allows me the time and space to write. She continues to amaze and inspire as an accomplished career educator with Job's patience, Esther's wisdom, and Ruth's tenacity!

Be blessed!

Wendell C Douglas

Introduction

Welcome, teacher, to this book about *"called"* teaching! This book will be the communication tool for me to share what I have learned from my multi-decade journey in education. What began as a young pastor's desire to serve a community as a volunteer coach and substitute teacher became the focus of my life's mission to "make a difference" in the world. I sincerely hope that by sharing what I've learned, I can help you find that same focus, passion, and fulfillment in your life's calling to teach. In the following pages, we will explore what it means to educate students from a called and practical perspective and how teachers can best fulfill their roles in this unique educational capacity. If you need a lifesaver or you are the one tossing it to a colleague, here it is! Be blessed!

From the start, teaching is a calling that requires unrelenting dedication, heartfelt passion, and a deep commitment to academic excellence and personal spiritual growth. Called educators have the challenge and unique opportunity to impart knowledge and skills and shape our students' hearts and minds, helping them develop a love for learning, a sense of purpose, and, even though subtle, a strong foundation in their faith. That is exciting!

James 3:1 (New Testament) reminds us that teaching is a called profession with blessings and accountability attached: "*My brothers and sisters, not many of you should become teachers because we know we will be judged more strictly*." I want to delve into various topics with you, including a little about called education philosophy, effective teaching strategies, classroom management techniques, curriculum development, and assessment and evaluation practices. I want to explore the challenges and rewards of called teaching, as well as the role of teachers in fostering a culture of community and service.

Following many years as a principal in public schools, I had the privilege of serving as the principal of three very different private schools, two of which were attached to specific church ministries and one faith-based but not sponsored by a specific church ministry. In my experiences, the people factors, including students, parents, church people, and the inevitable politics sometimes overshadowed the faith mission and purpose of the schools. The mission of the churches and their respective schools was often entangled and sometimes detrimental to progress. Communicating the entanglement to the church leadership was often tricky and nonproductive. However, administering an academic program in a "faith-based" school as part of a leadership team was much easier because there was no specific ministry to protect or promote. For me, a faith-based environment was more welcoming and inclusionary than those attached to the churches.

Thank you for letting me come along on this part of your journey! If you are a veteran teacher or just starting your teaching journey, I hope this book will provide some valuable insights and practical guidance for your *"called"* teaching journey. Together, we will explore what it means to educate with excellence and integrity, always keeping core faith values at the center of our classrooms and lives!

Chapter 1: The Calling

Early in my career, I discovered that teaching is not a job for the faint-hearted! Teaching is often considered a "calling" rather than just a job because, at many levels, it involves a deep commitment to serving students and families and a core desire to integrate deep-seated faith into every educational experience.

For many teachers (not all), the decision to is a response to a spiritual call on their lives. They feel a strong sense of purpose and mission to use their talents and abilities to nurture young people and to prepare them to become responsible, compassionate, and productive members of society.

Called teaching is not just about imparting knowledge. Along with academic excellence, it also involves creating a learning environment that reflects-however subtly- faith, love, and grace and encourages students to develop a deeper understanding of their place in the universe and their relationship with others.

Teaching is demanding, requiring dedication, sacrifice, and a willingness to serve others. But it is also a profoundly fulfilling and rewarding vocation, offering opportunities to impact students' lives and participate in the work of transforming the world. "Called" teachers try to uphold and model these values in teaching, interactions with students and parents, and relationships with colleagues integrating them into every subject and lesson. Are you still called?

Stable schools are often known for their strong sense of

community, where teachers, students, and families work together to create a supportive and nurturing learning environment and fellowship. As a teacher you will be expected to contribute to this community, building relationships with students, parents, and colleagues.

Schools are committed to academic excellence, and teachers are expected to deliver high-quality instruction that challenges and engages students. This teaching involves creating rigorous and relevant lesson plans, using effective strategies, and continually assessing and evaluating student progress. As a "called" school teacher, you must become a skilled master of your craft, knowledgeable, agile, and wholly committed to fulfilling your calling.

In addition to academic instruction, most schools also focus on character development, helping students to develop virtues such as honesty, integrity, kindness, and service. As a "called" teacher, you will be expected to model and promote these virtues and to provide opportunities for students to practice and develop them. Lesson planning, teaching strategies, and classroom management will be prime opportunities to showcase values and principles.

Suppose you are contemplating and even praying about teaching. It will be essential to consider the following questions as you reflect on your sense of calling and evaluate whether this spiritual vocation fits your gifts, skills, personality, and values.

Here is an opportunity for self-reflection on your calling to teach. Only you can answer each question on the checklist with honest intent. Seek divine guidance as you respond.

Respond by circling your best response on a scale of one to five, one being the lowest on the scale and five being the highest.

1=No 2 3= Not Decided 4 5=Absolutely!

Do you feel called to serve the community and others through teaching? 1 2 3 4 5

Are you committed to helping students develop a deeper understanding of themselves and their place in life? 1 2 3 4 5

Do you have a passion for young people and helping them to grow intellectually, socially, and spiritually? 1 2 3 4 5

Are you patient, compassionate, and able to build strong relationships with students, parents, and colleagues? 1 2 3 4 5

Are you willing to collaborate with other teachers, administrators, and staff to contribute to a positive and supportive school culture? 1 2 3 4 5

Do you have strong communication, organizational, and problem-solving skills and can adapt to different learning styles and abilities? 1 2 3 4 5

Are you willing to commit to ongoing professional development to improve your teaching practice? 1 2 3 4 5

Are you comfortable with the school's beliefs and values, and do you feel called to support and promote these values in your teaching? 1 2 3 4 5

Total Score _____/40

So, are you called to teach? Keep reading! As you reflect on your honest responses to these questions, you can better understand your sense of *calling* to teach and evaluate whether this vocation aligns with your gifts, passions, beliefs, and goals.

Chapter 2: Practical Things To Know: My Story

My friend, there are *essential* things and *critical* things that you'll need to know about teaching. Here's how my education about education came about...

I started college with no clue of what my life journey was to be. The Vietnam War was raging; the draft was in full swing, and a college deferment was a more sought-after piece of paper than was a diploma. By the time I won the draft lottery (the only thing I've ever won in my life), President Nixon had facilitated the U.S. exit from the war, and the deferment pressure had subsided a bit. I did manage to squeeze four years of college into six and a half years, with more drops and adds, major changes, and redirects than anyone in the world. I kept searching for purpose and direction.

Marriage, finishing school, entering the ministry, and starting a little church happened almost simultaneously. When my wife and I moved to the community where the little church started, she became a second-grade teacher in the school there. Substitute teaching at the school helped me find the passion and focus that would define my life. I finished my undergraduate work with a double major in social studies and speech education! I couldn't wait to get started making a difference!

After several interviews, I was offered my first teaching position during the oil boom in South Louisiana. I remember accepting the position, offered just as I completed student teaching, with a sense of pride and importance I'd never known. I was, at last, a teacher. It was like Christmas.

The classes I was assigned included American History, Civics, Economics, and Study Hall. I would be replacing a veteran teacher retiring at mid-term. Another teacher, retiring after a long tenure of service, gave me her parting advice as she prepared to exit the profession: "Mr. Douglas," she said in a low, calm tone. "I have two pieces of unasked-for advice. First, speak softly... don't yell...so they'll have to listen to hear you. Secondly, you'll have to find them before you can lead them."

"I've got this," I stupidly thought, graciously thanking her for her words of wisdom. Holding tightly the key to the door to *my* classroom, I quietly entered what seemed like my second-floor chamber of horrors. That January Friday afternoon, the room was dark, smelled funny, and the desks, books, and the teacher's desk were in utter disarray. I remember thinking, "The maintenance crew just hasn't cleaned yet."

The following Monday was the beginning of my real education about education. I quickly discovered that much of what I had learned in college about teaching could be scrapped. I also learned that mispronouncing the names of high school students is akin to insulting someone's mother. Just calling roll seemed like the challenge of a lifetime.

First-hour students shoved through the door, eying me up suspiciously as I waited.

"Who the @#$% is this?" one asked aloud to no one in particular.

"Must be a substitute," a nameless voice answered.
"Nope, he's our new teacher," someone chimed in.
"Is he gay or straight? Straight."
"Where's he from?"
"He drives a Mazda. I saw him in the parking lot."

This whole conversation reset and replayed at every class exchange that first day. For this, I sweated the draft; too many college credits, and only the Lord knows how much tuition.

As I glanced at the first-hour class, I realized that a couple of the kids were from the youth group at the church where I was pastor. The most interesting thing about them was that they completely ignored me, preferring to remain anonymous in that setting. I didn't blame them. I would have chosen anonymity, too.

As the day wore on, I interrupted a suspicious cigarette-rolling pursuit, encouraged a student to stop soliciting names from the class for her unborn child, and discreetly quashed a front-row gentleman's under-the-desktop activities.

I need to share with you that I bailed at the end of that Spring semester. I walked away from teaching. A church "called" me to be their youth minister, nearly doubled my salary, and the embarrassing foray into high-school education was left behind...but only temporarily. A calling is a calling. I had to learn the difference between a calling, an escape, an opportunity, and a temptation...but that's another story! I returned to teaching in the Fall of that same year...and I've never looked back.

Chapter 3: Plan For Success And Then Measure It!

I slowly realized that college doesn't prepare one for teaching. Nope. So, I'll be sharing with you some practical things to know and some critical things to know. Spoiler alert! You may have to figure out which one is which.

I taught Social Studies that first half-year. Although I had taken many social studies classes in preparation for teaching, I had NO CLUE about how to teach that content to students, much less what strategies to use in that sometimes impossible task. My excellent student-teaching mentor provided the teacher modeling that served him well in his classrooms. My best effort was to try to emulate his style. But in my classroom, with no mentor present, I'm sure my best efforts fell far short of his example and guidance!

So, in the real world of my classroom and the feverish quest to fulfill my calling, I stumbled into a jarring reality: Lesson planning is a key part of effective teaching and practical strategizing! Lesson Plan books and templates, both paper-pencil and online formats, are usually provided by schools, checked periodically by administrators or lead teachers, and are considered in job performance evaluations. Lesson plans are not only required; they become your best friend, your guiding light when things get foggy, and your reminder that you are progressing in delivering content!

Here are some basics of lesson planning. I learned "about" lesson planning in methods classes. I learned the "how" and the "why" in the real world. You start by identifying in no uncertain terms "what" you want your students to know or be able to do by the end of the lesson, focusing on one or two main learning objectives, to ensure the new knowledge and tasks are coherent and meaningful.

Just as important as the "what" of the lesson, you must be clear on "how" the lesson will be delivered. You get to choose appropriate materials and activities that you will have prepared for use in the lesson. You can select materials and activities aligned with your learning objectives but, most importantly, suitable for your student's age, level, and interests. Many resources are available, including various online materials and activities, including videos, images, handouts, games, and interactive exercises...limited only by your imagination and student interests! A word of caution: DO NOT ask students to do free-lance Googling of concepts online. I strongly encourage you to have preselected URLs available and closely monitor online activity. I hope you won't ask me how I discovered this little piece of wisdom. Some students will remember the fun lesson but have no clue about "what" should be learned!

Learning Assessment

A wise, experienced teacher once told me her assessment philosophy, "If it's worth teaching, it's worth testing. If you teach it, test it. If you don't teach it, don't test it." The bottom line is that you must plan how you will assess your students' learning and teach them how and when they will be assessed...even through activities like Kahoot, simple hand-raising, or a quick quiz. This can include formative assessments (including informal strategies) during the lesson and more formal summative assessments at the end of the lesson, nine weeks or a semester. Following the advice of my wise, experienced educator-friend, be sure to align your assessments with your learning objectives. If it's worth teaching, it's worth testing.

Kids Learn the Way They Learn

Students learn the way they learn, but not necessarily how they are taught. I learned this the hard way. My experience as a high school and college student had been that content delivery was monolithic, primarily in a "my way or the highway" atmosphere. Students were expected to adapt and adhere to the teacher's teaching style rather than the teacher adapting to the student's learning style.

Here's something essential to remember when planning your lessons and learning assessments. Consider your students' different needs and learning styles and prepare for differentiation to ensure all students can learn and succeed. This might include providing different levels of challenge, using other materials, or offering extra support or time to complete a task.

Make friends with your timer. In your lesson planning, ensure you have enough time to cover all the material and allow for informal checking for understanding and reflection. You will want to consider how long each activity will take and plan accordingly. Be prepared to adjust your plan if necessary. Flexibility is your best ally in a classroom. If an activity is not working or if students need more time to grasp a concept, be willing to make adjustments on the fly. Flexibility is a strength, not a weakness!

Learning Goals and Objectives

In visiting classrooms across the country for the past several years, I realized that even though various schools and districts have different formats and requirements for posting them, learning goals and objectives are essential to effective lesson planning and content delivery. Goals and objectives are usually tied to state standards and provide a roadmap for what you want your students need to know and how you will assess their learning.

I'm about to share another lesson I learned along the way. Here's a breakdown of the difference between teaching goals and objectives: *Learning goals* describe what you want your students to accomplish over a lesson, unit, or course. Goals are often written in general terms and focus on the overarching concepts or themes you want your students to understand. Goals should be relevant to your students' lives and connect to your curriculum and learning standards. For example, a goal might be to help students develop critical thinking skills or to teach students about the importance of environmental sustainability, etc.

Don't get confused. To this day, I can hear the same tune playing in my head...*Learning objectives* aligned to learning goals are specific, measurable, and time-referenced statements describing what your students want to achieve by the end of a lesson or unit. Objectives should focus on a particular skill or concept knowledge and align with your teaching goals. Objectives should be written in clear, concise language and should be achievable within the timeframe of the lesson or unit.

For example, an objective might be to help students identify and describe the characteristics of different plants, demonstrate knowledge of the colors of the rainbow, etc.

Remember, students learn the way they learn. When writing teaching goals and objectives, it's essential to consider your student's learning needs and abilities. Setting realistic and achievable goals and objectives to challenge them while providing opportunities for success for each one would be optimal for teaching and learning.

Remember to align your goals and objectives with your curriculum and learning standards to ensure students meet the required learning outcomes. You are helping the students and yourself design a roadmap for teaching and learning success! This feels good at the end of a busy and exhausting day! Your "calling" is unfolding!

Data-driven Planning

Student data is critical because making educated guesses is reserved for game shows, not education! If student data is used for nothing else, it must be the bellwether of teaching and learning effectiveness.   Using data to plan lessons is an effective way to tailor your teaching to meet the needs of your students. So where do you start?

You'll have to do some homework. Start by collecting available data on your student's progress and learning needs. This might include summative assessment results, standardized test scores, and student behavior and performance observations by previous teachers. Visit and analyze this data periodically to identify student learning patterns and trends.

Based on your data analysis, set clear and measurable learning goals for your students aligned with your curriculum and learning standards. Use your data analysis to plan targeted instruction and grouping strategies that address students' learning needs. This might involve using different teaching strategies or providing additional support for struggling students, usually best accomplished in small group settings. Use your data to differentiate instruction and provide different levels of support and challenge to meet the needs of all students. This might involve providing additional resources or activities for students performing at a high level or providing extra support and scaffolding for struggling students. Teach to mastery, not to artificial timelines.

You will want to use continuous formative assessments to monitor students' progress and adjust your instruction. This might involve using quizzes, exit tickets, or other informal assessments to gauge students' understanding and identify areas where they need additional support. Make it fun for yourself and the students as you gain valuable insights into their learning progress. This is "called" teaching! Students succeed...and so do you! It feels good.

A final note about lesson planning... After teaching your lesson, reflect on its effectiveness in meeting your learning goals. Use this feedback to adjust your instruction for future lessons. By using data to plan your lessons, you can plan your teaching to meet the specific needs of your students and provide them with the academic support and resources they will need to be successful. This will help to improve student focus, engagement, motivation, and achievement. Effective lesson planning takes reflective practice; remember that sometimes, the best-intentioned lessons fall apart. Don't despair; we've all been there. You are *called* to teach!

Chapter 4: Those Pesky Records

I must share another hard-learned lesson: Record-keeping is a practical and essential component of effective teaching. In my early days of teaching, I had recurring nightmares about being called into a parent conference and I had no gradebook, attendance record, or anything on paper to share with the parents! In most schools, this sometimes-daunting task is a major job requirement! For a teacher, it involves keeping accurate and up-to-date records of student progress, behavior, attendance, and more! So, we make record-keeping our friend and partner in our quest to help students be successful...and for us to remain employed!

By keeping records of student performance on assessments (formal and informal), you can do real-time progress monitoring and identify areas where they need additional support. This information will support your decision-making when differentiating learning, help you adjust your teaching, and provide targeted support for individuals or groups of students. The gradebook (online or paper pencil) is a great repository of formal and informal assessment progress. I would also encourage a private notebook of students' interests and hobbies to facilitate meaningful conversations with students, completely unattached to grades and academics.

Accurate record-keeping can help you to communicate with all stakeholders about their child's progress and behavior. Parents will generally want to see grades, behavior patterns, and trends; good record-keeping facilitates good communication. By sharing this information regularly, you can help parents be informed and actively involved in their child's education. No surprises.

Many schools and districts require teachers to maintain certain records to comply with state and federal reporting requirements. By maintaining accurate and timely records, you can ensure that you meet these requirements and provide the necessary information to administrators and other stakeholders. Keeping records of your students' achievements and accomplishments can help you document and see their progress over time. This can be useful for celebrating student achievement and identifying areas for additional support.

Accurate record-keeping can help you to manage your classroom more effectively. By keeping student behavior and attendance records, you can quickly spot patterns and trends and adjust your teaching or management strategies accordingly.

Teaching: Records and Confidentiality
Confidentiality is an essential consideration for teachers when working with students. Teachers must maintain the confidentiality of student information to protect the privacy and well-being of their students.

Familiarize yourself with the laws and policies governing student information confidentiality in your school or district. This may include federal laws such as FERPA and state or local regulations. You may want to do an internet search on the laws which govern where you teach and for which you'll be responsible.

You will want to collect and store only the information needed for teaching and learning. Be mindful of the types of information you collect and ensure it is relevant to your instructional goals. Always be mindful to store student information securely to prevent unauthorized access. This may involve keeping paper records in a locked cabinet or using a secure digital platform to store electronic records.

Share student information only with those who have a legitimate *need to know*. This may include administrators, other teachers, and parents or guardians. Explain why the information is necessary and how it will be used. Before sharing confidential information about a student with a third party, obtain written consent from parents or guardians. Be mindful of your behavior when discussing student information and avoid discussing student information in public or with those who do not have a legitimate need to know. Seek guidance from your school or district administrators if you have any questions about the confidentiality of student information. They can provide advice on specific policies and procedures related to student privacy.

WENDELL C DOUGLAS

Chapter 5: Teaching Strategies...What Are Those?

Embarking on a journey that spanned years, my career in education has been a tapestry woven with experience, growth, and transformation to say the least! It wasn't until later in my professional life that I stumbled upon the transformative world of innovative teaching strategies. Reflecting on my early years, where I predominantly relied on traditional straight lectures to deliver content, I feel the need to apologize to my students! I now realize the untapped potential that lay hidden within alternative, research-based, and effective teaching methodologies.

The revelation came for me as a beacon of change, illuminating a path toward more engaging, student-centered approaches. Discovering the power of interactive discussions, hands-on activities, and technology integration, I witnessed a profound shift in my classroom dynamics. Students became active participants, eager to explore, question, and connect the dots in ways that had previously eluded them during my lecture-dominated days.

As I immersed myself in this newfound knowledge, I couldn't help but wonder how different my early years could have been had I possessed these insights back then. The impact on student comprehension, retention, and enthusiasm was undeniable. It was as if a door had swung open to reveal an educational landscape brimming with possibilities, where learning was a collaborative adventure rather than a passive absorption of information.

My journey from traditional lectures to dynamic teaching strategies has taught me that evolution is an inherent aspect of education. While I can't rewrite the past, I am committed to championing these innovative methodologies in the present and future. Every day, I strive to make a difference, ensuring that the educators of tomorrow won't have to wait until later in their careers to uncover the transformative potential of varied teaching strategies.

Teaching Strategies refer to a set of techniques and methods educators use to facilitate learning in students. Teachers can use various teaching strategies in different settings, including classrooms, online learning platforms, and vocational training centers to facilitate teaching and learning. This chapter provides an overview of some of the most commonly used teaching strategies, and reference resources to explore further.

Active Learning

Be ready for what will appear to be chaos at first, but remember...active learning is active! Active learning is a teaching strategy that emphasizes the participation and engagement of students in the learning process. This approach encourages students to actively participate in their learning by asking questions, working on group projects, and participating in discussions (Freeman et al., 2014). Active learning promotes critical thinking, problem-solving skills, and knowledge retention in students. The teachers and students who embrace active learning are creating a learning space that daily beckons an excited, engaged teacher and takes the boredom and tedium out of learning for students! There are tons of resources available to help you turn your classroom lessons into exciting and engaging learning journeys! Google "active learning" and hit print!

Collaborative Learning

Collaborative learning is a strategy that encourages students to work in groups to complete assignments or projects. This strategy emphasizes the importance of teamwork, communication, and social skills (Slavin, 2015). Students and teachers can do collaborative teaching and learning in person or online, and it promotes knowledge sharing, peer teaching, and collective problem-solving. By creating opportunities for teamwork, communication, and collective problem-solving, students can engage with peers, and explore a myriad of diverse perspectives. They also get to refine their interpersonal skills and expand their critical thinking horizons. Beyond knowledge acquisition, collaborative learning cultivates adaptability and empathy, essential traits for the modern world! One word of caution...keep the learning styles and personality traits of your students in mind as you design lessons that require interactivity with other students.

Inquiry-based learning

This strategy encourages students to ask questions and seek answers through research and exploration (Graesser et al., 2018). This approach emphasizes critical thinking, problem-solving, and discovery learning. Inquiry-based learning encourages exploring topics that interest them, and they can pursue them in a structured learning environment.

Inquiry-based learning empowers students tobe the architects of their own education, nurturing a deep-seated curiosity and a lifelong love for learning. I need to say right up front that this method is not for everyone. The student who, for what ever reasons, may not want to work with other students might benefit greatly from this teaching-learning strategy. By encouraging questions, exploration, and self-discovery, this approach seeks to fuel intellectual curiosity and critical thinking skills. As students formulate their own inquiries and seek answers, they become active participants in constructing knowledge, hopefully leading to understanding that goes beyond rote memorization. Through this method, students develop problem-solving skills, independence, and a sense of ownership over their learning journey. Used judiciously, inquiry-based learning equips students for academic success and nurtures their capacity to navigate the world of learning with confidence and an unquenchable thirst for knowledge.

Flipped Classroom

A flipped classroom is a strategy that involves "flipping" the traditional classroom model, where students watch pre-recorded lectures or lessons before coming to class and then use class time for discussions, group activities, and hands-on projects (Bergmann & Sams, 2012). The flipped classroom model facilitates students learning at their own pace, and it emphasizes the importance of active learning and student engagement.

I saw this strategy used often in M1 and M2 medical education classrooms. Flipped classroom learning changes the educational experience by reversing traditional roles, placing students at the forefront of their own learning journey. In this approach, students engage with instructional content at their own pace outside of class, often through videos or readings. This paves the way for valuable in-class time to be dedicated to active discussions, collaborative projects, and personalized guidance from teachers. Using this approach with older, more responsible students seems a better match than younger, less independent learners in primary grades.

Take a look at the benefits for the students who can successfully participate in the flipped classroom experience. They gain autonomy over their learning process, and mastering foundational concepts before class discussions deepen their understanding. Collaborative activities foster peer-to-peer interaction, enhancing communication skills and teamwork. Furthermore, the personalized attention from the teacher during in-class sessions allows for targeted support, ensuring no student is left behind. This is huge!

Flipped classroom learning not only promotes deeper comprehension of subject matter but also equips students with time management skills, critical thinking abilities, and a proactive approach to learning. However, be warned...this strategy requires throughly thought-through planning and preparation for the experience to be successful for you the teacher as well as your students. Worth a try? You bet!

Modeling

Modeling is an effective teaching strategy that involves demonstrating or modeling a skill or concept for students to observe and imitate. Reading lessons, math, you name it...students who need to "see" the lesson unfold in steps benefit significantly by watching the teacher model learning for them.

Again, a word of caution...If you inadvertently mess up, don't berate yourself for making a mistake. Students will also "learn" this negative response and internalize the negative self-appraisal that you're modeling.

Here are a few helpful suggestions for using modeling with your students, based on the *"I do, we do, you do"* approach that we've all heard so much about in the gradual release approach to teaching and learning.

I do: Before modeling, identify the specific skill or concept you want to teach. Make sure it aligns with your learning objectives and the needs of your students. Demonstrate the skill or concept for your students through a live demonstration or video recording. Explain each step and provide examples of correct and incorrect ways to perform the skill. After demonstrating the skill or concept, allow students time to observe and take notes. Always encourage students to ask questions and seek more information if needed.

We do: After modeling the lesson, provide students with guided practice opportunities to try out the skill or concept with your support and guidance. Make sure to give feedback and correct errors as needed. Once students have had guided practice, provide opportunities for independent practice. Encourage students to independently apply the skill or concept and provide feedback as needed.

You do: After you've modeled and they've practiced, you'll want to provide opportunities for them to demonstrate their understanding. These may include quizzes, projects, or other assessment. Be creative and make it fun...for them, and for you!

Teaching in Small Groups

Because all students don't learn the same way, at the same time, and at the same level, differentiated learning is the name of the game. It has been for ages, but maybe just not called that. "A rose by any other name..." Eons ago, reading groups were labeled "Redbirds" "Bluebirds" and "Sparrows"...all designed to teach reading and math in differentiated groups.

Small group instruction requires a lot of planning to be effective. In your small group planning, be sure you have clear learning objectives for the lesson and that you have chosen the suitable activities and materials to support those objectives. Students come to class with different backgrounds, experiences, and abilities.

Small group instruction allows for more opportunities for individual participation (as you observe and support), formative assessment, and specific feedback. As I was observing in a fourth grade classroom one day, time came for small groups to move to their locations. The student seated nearest me leaned over and whispered, "I like small group. It's the only time I get to talk to my teacher." Duly noted.

Chapter 6: It's All About Style!

I don't remember when I learned about learning styles and the incredible impact an understanding of how students learn has on classroom teaching and faculty meetings! Everyone has a preferred learning style but generally adapted to other styles when necessary to do so. Public speakers (preachers and politicians included!) would do well to embrace these learning styles to capitalize on the processing of their messages by their audiences!

Effective teaching strategies are intertwined with the learning styles of students. Every student has a distinctive way of learning, which can significantly impact their academic performance. Learning styles refer to individuals' preferred methods of receiving, processing and retaining information.

What's your compelling cause to understand learning preferences? Teachers who understand their students' learning styles can then tailor their teaching strategies to accommodate each student's needs, creating an inclusive and effective learning environment. In this way, teachers need to identify their students' learning styles to design appropriate teaching strategies that enhance their learning outcomes. How can this be done? By intentionally constructing listening components, visual pieces, reading and writing components, and kinesthetic (movement) components in most lessons, you touch on each learning preference and create a gateway for new learning. Google "learning styles" and a plethora of information will appear. While some terminology may differ from one source to another, the information is solid and the mandate for teaching and learning is clear. Here are a few tips to remember:

The visual learning preference is best suited for students who enjoy visualizing and conceptualizing concepts in their "mind's eye." Visual learners prefer to process information through pictures, diagrams, and videos, and re-creations. Visual learners are adept at taking notes and creating mind maps to organize information.

The auditory learning preference manifests as processing information through sound, such as lectures, discussions, and audio recordings. This learning style is preferred by students who learn best through listening and discussing concepts with others. Auditory learners tend study and read aloud and excel at remembering verbal information and reciting information aloud. Reading silently for an auditory processor is usually a time suck.

Kinesthetic learners want hands-on experiences and physical activities to make learning a memorable experience. Kinesthetic learners are good at memorizing information through physical activity and movement. They become great dancers who remember all the moves...and lyrics!

Multi-modal learners are those learners who tend to be flexible and adaptable to different learning situations. They are able to process learning through whatever means necessary, with little to no preference for one particular learning style over another.

So what is the purpose for knowing about learning strategies and learning styles? Understanding students' learning styles, including visual, auditory, kinesthetic, and multimodal learners, is vital in designing instructional methods anf strategies to match their learning preferences.

Teachers who employ various teaching strategies and recognize students' learning styles create an inclusive learning environment that promotes student engagement, retention, and academic success. Search online for information about this critical topic to help determine your students' learning styles. While searching, look for ways to weave practical teaching strategies and learning styles together for effective teaching and learning. You'll enjoy the experience of engaged learning as much as the students!

Chapter 7: Managing Your Classroom

When you don't know a student's name, trying to influence their thinking and behavior is almost impossible (and nearly laughable). The truth is "classroom management" is a by-product of relationship management. When you establish a relationship, beginning with learning a child's name, you've cracked the door to influence possibilities, banishing anonymity. Building relationships- and daily nurturing those relationships- makes a lasting difference in a student's life. Because of those relationships, teachers become trusted life guides for children and earn the right to influence thoughts, behaviors, and lives.

Teachers are classroom managers only if they are effective relationship managers. The real influencers learn names, build and nurture relationships, and help guide lives. Furniture and desks can easily be "managed," but growing lives takes a little more work. Relationship management in a school classroom will likely involve techniques and methods to promote positive behaviors, discipline, and academic success in students while aligning with community-building values and beliefs. The key difference between a facilitative teacher and a coercive teacher is this... Facilitative teachers elicit the best from students using wisdom, insight, self-discipline, discernment, and integrity. Coercive 'teachers' do not. Facilitative teachers manage relationships. Coercive teachers do not.

My friend, be sure you have an arsenal of positive techniques ready! Communicating and maintaining behavior expectations in a classroom requires a thoughtful and meaningful approach that reflects ethical values while promoting a positive learning environment. Examine the "what" and "why" of your expectations and then use the most effective (positive) way of communicating them to your students. Of course, by incorporating ethical values into your behavior expectations, you can create a positive and nurturing classroom environment that fosters the growth and development of your students' character and social skills. You'll also create a welcoming and inclusive classroom culture that encourages students to respect each other's differences and fosters a sense of community, emphasizing the importance of kindness, empathy, and forgiveness in your classroom.

Classroom Rules and Procedures

How do you start? Communicate your behavior expectations to your students, including collaborative rules and consequences. A creative and eye-catching bulletin board is a great place to post your expectations for classroom interactions. The bulletin board would also be a great place to communicate the nonnegotiable nature of your behavior expectations. Once you've created them, teach them.

As a teacher, always remember that nothing replaces clear communication. If you have fifteen or thirty students in your classroom, the potential for misunderstanding is as great as your number of students multiplied by the number of people with whom they interact! Because you are a *called* teacher, use rules and procedures that align with the values of honesty, integrity, and responsibility. These may include guidelines for respectful communication with other students and teachers, caring for others, and following the school's code of conduct.

Classroom rules and procedures are a classroom management strategy that establishes clear expectations for student behavior (Marzano & Pickering, 2005). You may need to explain why your behavior expectations are essential and nonnegotiable and how they align with your classroom values.

I quickly learned the worth of the list I'm sharing with you. My first four years in school administration were at a middle school, and my primary job every day was to handle disciplinary referrals. Where these classroom elements were present, referrals were lower in number.

There are some essential elements of an effective management plan for classroom discipline. These are rudimentary to a solid plan and part of a broader purpose. You may add to the list as you see fit or as deemed appropriate by your school's code of behavior. Remember, you want a just, kind, respectful, welcoming, and inclusive atmosphere in your classroom.

Here are some impactful strategies to incorporate into your overall classroom plan for student behavior management:

Establish clear expectations and then teach them; let there be no room for misunderstandings!

Be consistent; management by mood does not work in a classroom.

Address misbehavior promptly; other students are watching, and learning time is wasting!

Use consequences appropriately and consistently; never react...pause and respond.

Try to be empathetic; we were that age once upon a time.

Never promise or threaten what you can't deliver; never.

Build positive relationships with students; look for opportunities to improve a child's life, if just for a day.

Modeling

As a *called* teacher, you can serve as a behavior role model for your students. Demonstrate the expected behaviors you want to see in your students, such as patience, kindness, and forgiveness. Proceed with caution. Remember that students, professional peers, parents, and the community are watching. And we already know that a cell phone or another device continuously records our every word and deed!

Appropriate Positive Reinforcement

I mentioned *positive reinforcement* in the list above and wanted to elaborate a little here. Positive reinforcement is a classroom management strategy that involves rewarding students for positive behaviors and achievements (Freiberg, 2016). Although you will need to use the rewards and systems that work best for your classroom, positive reinforcement can include something as simple as a thumbs up, verbal praise, certificates of achievement, and other rewards tailored to the school's values. A word of caution here: Do not get trapped into "buying" appropriate behavior!

Let me quickly say that your positive reinforcement efforts must be age, gender, and "touch" appropriate, always asking for permission to hug, high-five, or pat on the back. Likewise, overly complementing a student in front of their peers can cause them to become resented by peers quickly. Schools often use positive reinforcement techniques that align with their values, such as rewarding students for acts of kindness, sharing, and other value-driven behaviors.

Restorative Justice

Restorative justice is a classroom management strategy that focuses on repairing the harm caused by negative behaviors rather than punishing students (Zehr, 2015). This approach emphasizes the importance of making amends and restoring relationships rather than solely punishing students for their misbehavior. Restorative justice techniques align with the social values of forgiveness, compassion, and reconciliation.

There is a great temptation to punish students for misconduct and to leave it to them to figure out a way back. Punishment as a long term approach to behavior management simply does not work. Our criminal justice system stands as proof. A punishment-only approach can scar a student's sense of self-worth and value to the classroom community. In the event of misconduct, which is inevitable, you can practice restorative justice by emphasizing forgiveness, reconciliation, and accountability.

When to Involve Parents in Behavior Issues

As a classroom teacher, you must have a good relationship with parents and guardians. They expect you to be kind to their children, honest with them, and help them grow academically and socially toward maturity.

I discovered an interesting truth during my first year as an Assistant Principal in charge of school discipline. Involving parents in student behavior issues is an important decision to be made carefully and thoughtfully. Getting parents involved with minor, inconsequential transgressions can potentially diminish their view of your classroom management skills and professionalism.

Here are some tips I've collected for *when* to involve parents in student behavior issues:

When the behavior poses a safety risk: If a student's behavior poses a safety risk to themselves or others;

When a student's behavior is consistently disruptive to the learning environment; You can't teach and they can't learn;

When a student's behavior is a violation of school policies or rules; and

When a student's behavior affects their academic performance and learning ability.

By involving parents in student behavior issues when necessary, you can work together to address the behavior and prevent future incidents while promoting a positive and collaborative relationship between home and school. It is essential to involve parents promptly and respectfully while respecting the privacy and confidentiality of all involved. One point of advice would be to have a game plan in mind and clearly ask for the kind of support you need from the parents or guardians to help the student succeed. ***Having a meeting with parents without a plan to move forward is a non-starter and very counterproductive.***

Special Needs Students in the Classroom

Special needs students require unique support and accommodations in the classroom to help them succeed academically, socially, and emotionally. Understanding the student's needs is the first step to providing adequate support. You, the classroom teacher, must learn about the student's individualized education plan (IEP) or 504 plan, which outlines the student's specific needs and accommodations, and work closely with the student's support team.

If you are to be blessed with a Special Needs student in your classroom, creating a supportive learning environment that accommodates the student's needs will be crucial. This may include adaptations to the classroom environment, such as specialized seating or lighting, or additional support, such as a teaching assistant.

You will likely already be using differentiated instruction to meet the needs of all students in the classroom, and this approach will also include instruction for special needs students as well. Differentiated instruction (small group) may involve adapting instructional methods, materials, or assessment strategies to meet students' needs.

Special Needs students present you with great opportunities to foster positive relationships with not only the students and their support team but also parents, counselors, and other professionals. A positive approach can help to create a supportive and collaborative learning environment and promote the student's (and the rest of the class's) social and emotional well-being. You may need to provide accommodations and modifications that support the student's learning, such as assistive technology, additional time for assignments or assessments, or a modified curriculum. Explore all possibilities! Your best resources for help may be the parents themselves.

By effectively teaching and supporting special needs students in your classroom, you can help create a positive and supportive learning environment that promotes all students' academic, social, and emotional well-being. By understanding the student's needs and teaching accordingly, you can provide a rich and rewarding experience for you and everyone in your classroom!

Chapter 8: Curriculum Development. Jump In!

My first principalship at a private religious school was a startling awakening for me. After many years in public school administration, where curriculum, state mandates, and best practices dominated the expectations for each district and campus, I became the principal of a small private school with close ties to the ministry that began the school.

The vision of the affiliated ministry was to move the school forward as quickly as possible to state accreditation and recognition. A great desire to see students succeed seemed pervasive at the school, but the organizational structures to move the school toward state accreditation were not in place. Recruiting and hiring state-certified teachers in tandem with creating a cohesive and coherent K-12 curriculum that met state accreditation mandates and properly empowered students were no small tasks.

As a faculty team, we learned much about state requirements for accredited schools in our state; we learned so much more about the ability of *called* teachers to accomplish the improbable...and the nearly impossible!. I want to share with you, my teacher friend, some of the curriculum-related things we learned along the way and why those things are necessary to meet the needs of students.

College and Career Readiness

Now more than ever, college and career readiness for students is essential for all schools, including faith-based schools. Private schools must offer rigorous academic lessons that prepare students to consider college and career success. As a teacher, always be aware of college and career readiness plans that outline the goals, strategies, and tactics for promoting college and career readiness among all students, even lower elementary students!

Additionally, as a *called* classroom teacher, you'll be able to encourage students to participate in extracurricular activities that build leadership, teamwork, and communication skills and demonstrate their commitment and passion for their interests. Your classroom will provide a platform for you to promote service and social justice among students and help them to develop a sense of responsibility and compassion for others. Most importantly, you'll be able to help students find a sense of purpose and meaning and help them to connect their faith and values with their college and career aspirations.

I fully believe you can't know where you're going unless you know where you've been. At the school I mentioned earlier, developing a cohesive curriculum that prepared students for the next grade level had to begin with creating a school-wide, cross-grade level, collaborative learning environment. The curriculum had to intentionally and progressively integrate values, principles, and beliefs into every subject area. The former curriculum was primarily based on a popular Christian curriculum, but it seemed the school lacked the overall cohesive, intentional academic progression necessary for appropriate grade-level achievement.

The support of the affiliated church ministry staff was critical.

Even though aspects of the ministry were undergoing change and challenges, the mission was clear and pastoral support was solid in recruiting certified teachers and expeditiously moving the school toward state accreditation.

Now, my friend, suppose you are called upon to lead the charge of curriculum reform or alignment at your school. In that case, you'll first want to identify the principles aligning with your school's mission statement and vision. The school's mission and vision should be foundational to every facet of the school's life. Students and parents should have the mission and vision statements readily accessible, clearly communicated on the school's website and social media, and internalized by the faculty and staff of the school. Teachers and school leaders all have a stake in protecting and articulating the scope and integrity of the school's mission and vision statements. Mission and vision statements define the school's purpose, values, and goals.

Use the survey questions below to clarify where the school stands in light of these expectations. Of course, any of these questions could function as a focus for committee work or professional development.

YES   NO   IDK   Can we identify the school's purpose and define what the school hopes to achieve? *These may include statements about the school's educational philosophy, values, and goals.*

YES   NO   IDK   Can we identify the school's core values and principles that guide its operations and decision-making? *These may include statements about respect, inclusivity, academic excellence, and character development.*

YES   NO   IDK   Can we define the school's goals and objectives for student learning, teaching excellence, and community engagement? *These may include statements about academic achievement, student growth, and community partnerships.*

YES   NO   IDK   Do we use concise language that is easy to understand and effectively communicates the school's mission and values? *Avoid jargon or technical language that may be difficult for parents or community members to* *understand.*

YES   NO   IDK   Do we ensure that the school's actions align with the mission and vision statements? *The statements should be used as a guide for decision-making and reflected in the school's practices, policies, and procedures.*

YES   NO   IDK   Do we involve stakeholders, including teachers, parents, students, and community members, in creating the mission and vision statements? *This involvement can help ensure that the mission statement reflects the values and priorities of the entire school community.*

YES   NO   IDK   By identifying the school's purpose, core values, and goals, does our mission statement for our classrooms reflect the values and priorities of the school community?

YES   NO   IDK   Do we integrate Christian values into all subjects, such as science, math, and history? *For example, teach environmental stewardship in science, social justice in history, and ethical decision-making in business.*

YES   NO   IDK   Do we use a biblical worldview to guide curriculum development and instruction? *Help students understand how the Bible applies to all areas of life and how it shapes their understanding of the world.*

YES   NO   IDK   Do we engage in cross-curricular planning to ensure all subjects are interconnected and aligned with Christian values? *Work collaboratively with other teachers to develop interdisciplinary projects that demonstrate the integration of Christian principles into all subject areas.*

YES   NO   IDK   Do we use technology and media to enhance learning and reinforce Christian principles? *Incorporate relevant videos, podcasts, and other multimedia resources that illustrate Christian principles in action.*

YES   NO   IDK   Do we engage in professional development opportunities to learn about new teaching strategies, resources, and technologies that support the development of a cohesive curriculum? *Schools must provide relevant professional development to help teachers stay abreast of new information in the teaching and learning profession and to be able to translate new learning into relevance in the classroom.*

Prepared, *called* teachers can provide students with an education that prepares them for college or careers and a life of service, leadership, and faith.

Secondly, my friend, please remember that an effective curriculum is a cohesive curriculum. This checkup list will help you to reflect on your school's curriculum and practices.

*At the end of each question, you might insert the question **Why not?** or **What is our evidence?** The answers are essential.*

YES   NO   IDK   Does the school and each grade level have written curriculum objectives?

YES   NO   IDK   Do the curriculum objectives align with the school's mission and vision?

YES NO IDK Are the curriculum objectives challenging, relevant, and aligned with state and national standards?

YES   NO   IDK   Is there a clear progression of skills and knowledge from grade to grade, and are there opportunities for students to explore advanced topics?

YES NO IDK Are there clear expectations and plans for differentiated assistance for striving learners?

YES NO IDK Is student learning data used to inform and differentiate instruction?

YES   NO   IDK   Is there a program in place for foundational literacy instruction?

YES NO IDK Is there a program or plan to teach literacy across subject areas?

YES   NO   IDK   Do the curriculum objectives align with the school's mission and vision?

YES   NO   IDK   Are the curriculum objectives developmentally appropriate for the grade level?

YES NO IDK Is there a clear progression of skills and knowledge from grade to grade?

YES NO IDK Are school principles and values integrated into all subject areas?

YES   NO   IDK   Is there a consistent approach to teaching school principles and values across all grade levels and subject areas?

YES   NO   IDK   Is there evidence of cross-curricular planning and interdisciplinary projects integrating school principles and values into multiple subject areas?

YES   NO   IDK   Are there opportunities for students to apply school principles and values to real-world situations?

YES NO IDK Does the curriculum provide opportunities for students to develop character traits, such as empathy, compassion, and forgiveness?

YES   **NO**   **IDK**   Are assessments aligned with curriculum objectives,school values, and principles?

YES   **NO**   **IDK**   Is there a clear plan for measuring the effectiveness of the curriculum in promoting the school's values and principles?

YES   **NO**   **IDK**   Are parents and the wider community involved in supporting, developing, and implementing a cohesive curriculum?

YES   **NO**   **IDK**   Are teachers provided with professional development opportunities to enhance their knowledge and skills in developing and implementing a cohesive curriculum including technology and multimedia resources?

YES   **NO**   **IDK**   Will the curriculum adequately prepare students for college, career, and life?

Each of these questions potentially provides an opportunity for professional development and grade-level meetings for planning and reflection. You may be the one called upon to lead these explorations! This opportunity may be a subset of your calling to teach!

Chapter 9: A Final Word...For Now

Two of the greatest challenges of growing healthy children are helping them to filter out toxic criticism and teaching them to internalize life-enhancing, learning support and guidance. Be their advocate, safe place, and cheerleader... they all need one these days.

Whether you're a teacher, principal, parent, friend, or colleague, what you say matters to someone. When what you say matters... think before you assume, accuse, berate, or imply. When what you say matters, use your words to guide, heal, help, and inspire. Relationships are much too precious to ruin by needing to be right at any cost.

You don't gain respect and the right to influence students by disparaging those who've already achieved that status. Respect and the right to influence are earned through genuine relationships, not by demand, through fear, or by power of position.

As an elementary school principal, I often had to referee relationship squabbles, most of which had origins with one friend being ditched for another. My inevitable private go-to question to the sparring parties was, "If you met someone just like you, would you want to be best friends with them?" The "yes" answer opened the door for my "why" follow-up question. Of course, the "no" answer merited the same follow-up question. Both offered opportunities for introspective conversations...So, would you want to be a student with a teacher like you?

Aspire to be the boss who inspired YOU to productivity and job satisfaction. Aspire to be the administrator who inspired YOU to excellence. Aspire to be the teacher who inspired YOU to focus, try harder...to succeed.

————

Some of the most effective "instructional" words ever spoken to me came from my high school junior year English teacher... As she handed back an essay to me, she quietly said, "Was that your best? I expect more from you." .... Needless to say, the do-over essay was a step up...and the vote of confidence from her was never forgotten. Teaching. Learning.

————

Talking isn't teaching. The greatest responsibility for effective communication in a classroom lies with the speaker, not the listener. Clarity of language, message, and ascertaining understanding are all functions of message transmission not reception.

————

Student behavior redirection in a private conversation... "I care about you too much to let you think this is OK." and "You are better than this."

Differences are made when trust is the foundation of a student-teacher relationship.

————

Don't mistake silence for tacit approval. For a thinker, silence means that you'll get the best response and action after all possibilities have been considered. Rushing to judgment or jumping to conclusions is not what thinkers do.

————

Teaching without learning is just talking. Talking is not teaching.

————

When I took my motorcycle certification course, one guy asked the instructor, "How much should I pay for a helmet?" The instructor replied, "How much is your head worth?"

When it comes to hiring, paying, and retaining effective teachers...we have to ask, "How much is my child worth?"

————

A Note to my Teacher Friends

So here's the "it" of life...derived from life's wisdom in a sharp, retrospective view. Either we have "it" or we don't. One of the most unhealthy, self-imposed side effects of teaching, coaching, ministering, parenting, and befriending people takes hold when you assume responsibility for someone else's life decisions, behavior, and outcomes. Only an arrogant fool would try to claim someone else's success as their own. Likewise, only a fool would claim responsibility for someone else's failures when that failure resulted from someone else's decisions ... and then try to measure his own self-worth, success, and/or failures by theirs.

But sometimes that's exactly what we do! We teach so that students will solve problems like we do, write like we do, read like we do, and make good grades...like we did. Preachers preach so that people will behave themselves like they should, live like they should, pray like they should, and be living, giving examples of pastoral success. Parents trying to create 2.0 versions of themselves will meet with frustration and grief; grandparents trying to "advise" their way into re-creating their parenting roles will be met with disregard; and friends trying to create in others images of themselves will soon find themselves alone...and friendless.

So what's a loving, caring person to do? I suspect we should do what worked well for us as we developed into individual, independent thinkers and pursuers of life. Teach what you know to be true, understanding that each person must test "truth" for himself. Own the worst of your behavior and mistakes, but know that every person will assess your impact on them and will react to you accordingly. Love generously, with the realization that not everyone will love you back. Let go graciously, forgiving (yourself and others) to move on, forgetting when you can, focused forward.

Go do great things! You are called to a mighty task and you have the "it!" Find them, lead them, celebrate them. They are depending on you! Be blessed!

Dr. Wendell C Douglas, CEO-LearnTrax Education

ABOUT THE AUTHOR

Dr. Wendell C Douglas

 Certified Time To Teach! Trainer | Educational Consulting and Professional Development | Public School Administration/Leadership K-12 | Christian School Administration/Leadership K-12 | Medical Education Instructional Strategist – Research Support | Writer – Author | Master Certified Professional Life Coach | International Association of Professional Life Coaches | CEO LearnTrax Education, LLC

Further Reading and References

"Lesson Planning." https://cte.smu.edu.sg/approach-teaching/integrated-design/lesson-planning.

"A Checklist for Lesson Planning | Edutopia." 30 Jun. 2023, https://www.edutopia.org/article/checklist-lesson-planning.

"What Is a Lesson Plan and How Do You Make One?." 01 Sept. 2019, https://www.aeseducation.com/blog/what-is-a-lesson-plan.

"27+ Lesson Plan Examples & Templates for Effective Teaching [+ Writing Tip]." 29 May. 2023, https://venngage.com/blog/lesson-plan-examples/.

"How To Create A Lesson Plan: 6 Easy, Effective Steps." 21 Apr. 2022, https://educationadvanced.com/resources/blog/how-to-create-a-lesson-plan-6-easy-effective-steps/.

"30 Lesson Plan Examples for Every Grade and Subject." 03 Aug. 2023, https://www.weareteachers.com/lesson-plan-examples/.

"Browse Lesson Plans | Education.com." https://www.education.com/lesson-plans/.

"Formal and Informal Assessments." http://flbt5.floridaearlylearning.com/docs/dirtoolkit/3Formal%20and%20Informal%20Assessments.pdf.

"13 Creative Examples of Informal Assessments for the Classroom." 11 Jul. 2019, https://www.thoughtco.com/informal-classroom-assessments-4160915.

"Formal Assessment Vs. Informal Assessment: What's The Difference? - Zippia." 25 Oct. 2022, https://www.zippia.com/advice/formal-vs-informal-assessment/.

"Types of Informal Classroom-Based Assessment | Reading Rockets." https://www.readingrockets.org/topics/assessment-and-evaluation/articles/types-informal-classroom-based-assessment.

"Formal vs. Informal Assessment: 15 Key Differences & Similarities." 09 Aug. 2021, https://www.formpl.us/blog/formal-vs-informal-assessment.

"Basics: Informal Classroom-Based Assessment | Reading Rockets." https://www.readingrockets.org/reading-101/reading-and-writing-basics/informal-classroom-based-assessment.

"How Kids Learns - Focus on the Family." https://www.focusonthefamily.com/parenting/how-kids-learns/.

"How Children Learn - The National Academies Press." https://nap.nationalacademies.org/read/9853/chapter/7.

"The Way They Learn - amazon.com." 01 Apr. 1998, https://www.amazon.com/They-Learn-Cynthia-Ulrich-Tobias/dp/1561794147.

"How Kids Develop Cognitive Skills - Understood." https://www.understood.org/en/articles/how-kids-develop-thinking-and-learning-skills.

"Teach the Way They Learn Teaching Resources | Teachers Pay Teachers - TPT." https://www.teacherspayteachers.com/Store/Teach-The-Way-They-Learn.

"On Learning Goals and Learning Objectives - Derek Bok." https://bokcenter.harvard.edu/learning-goals-and-learning-objectives.

"Writing Effective Learning Goals - Center for Teaching and Learning." https://ctl.wustl.edu/resources/writing-effective-learning-goals/.

"Developing Learning Objectives | Center for Excellence in Teaching and learning" https://cetl.uconn.edu/resources/design-your-course/developing-learning-objectives/.

"The Difference Between Learning Goals & Learning Objectives | DDINC." 12 Apr. 2020, https://www.designingdigitally.com/blog/difference-between-employee-learning-goals-and-learning-objectives.

"Learning Objectives Basics - Center for Teaching and Learning | Wiley ...." 14 Jul. 2016, https://ctl.wiley.com/learning-objectives-basics/.

"The Power of Data: Instructional Strategies to Help You Create a Data ...." 30 Oct. 2018, https://betterlesson.com/blog/data-driven-classroom.

"Using Data-Driven Instruction in Your Classroom." 29 Apr. 2019, https://blog.advancementcourses.com/articles/data-driven-instruction/.

"Data-Driven Lesson Planning Professional Development - LearningFront." https://www.learningfront.com/mergenthaler/pages/pd_letter.html.

"Week 5 Benchmark Data Driven Lesson Planning.docx - Running...." https://www.coursehero.com/file/52475397/Week-5-Benchmark-Data-Driven-Lesson-Planningdocx/.

"The Ultimate Guide to Data-Driven Instruction (2023) | Otus." https://otus.com/guides/data-driven-instruction/.

"Record Keeping Tips For Teachers | Record Nations." https://www.recordnations.com/articles/record-keeping-teachers/.

"The Importance of Record Keeping in Your Classroom." 21 Feb. 2019, https://microrecord.com/blog/importance-record-keeping-classroom/.

"Housekeeping and Record Keeping Tasks for Teachers - ThoughtCo." 06 Mar. 2017, https://www.thoughtco.com/teacher-housekeeping-tasks-8393.

"The Educator's Role: Privacy, Confidentiality, and Security in the ...." 19 Nov. 2019, https://studentprivacycompass.org/scheid1/.

"The Case for Including Data Privacy and Data Ethics in Educator ...." 05 Oct. 2021, https://studentprivacycompass.org/resource/case-data-privacy-ethics/.

"Family Educational Rights and Privacy Act (FERPA)." 25 Aug. 2021, https://www2.ed.gov/policy/gen/guid/fpco/ferpa/index.html.

"The School Counselor and Confidentiality - American School Counselor ...." https://www.schoolcounselor.org/Standards-Positions/Position-Statements/ASCA-Position-Statements/The-School-Counselor-and-Confidentiality.

"Understanding the Confidentiality Requirements Applicable to IDEA Early ...." 28 Sept. 2011, https://studentprivacy.ed.gov/sites/default/files/resource_document/file/idea-confidentiality-requirements-faq_0.pdf.

https://www.purdue.edu/activelearning/Need_20Help/alstrategies.php
https://ctl.columbia.edu/resources-and-technology/teaching-with-technology/teaching-online/active-learning/

Marzano, R. J., & Pickering, D. J. (2005). Classroom management that works: Research-based strategies for every teacher. ASCD.

Zehr, H. (2015). The Little Book of Restorative Justice. Good Books.

Bergmann, J., & Sams, A. (2012). *Flip your classroom: Reach every student in every class every day.* International Society for Technology in Education.

Freeman, S., Eddy, S. L., McDonough, M., Smith, M. K., Okoroafor, N., Jordt, H., & Wenderoth, M. P. (2014). *Active learning increases student performance in science, engineering, and mathematics.* Proceedings of the National Academy of Sciences, 111(23), 8410-8415.

Graesser, A. C., Jeon, M., & Dufty, D. F. (2018). *Agent technologies for promoting meaningful learning in inquiry-based science classrooms.* Journal of Educational Psychology, 110(1), 26-43.

Slavin, R. E. (2015). *Cooperative learning and academic achievement: Why does groupwork work?* Anales de Psicología, 31(3), 785-797.

Felder, R. M., & Silverman, L. K. (1988). *Learning and teaching styles in engineering education.* Engineering Education, 78(7), 674-681.

VARK Learning Styles (vark-learn.com)
Kolb, D. A. (2014). *Experiential learning: Experience as the source of learning and development.* FT Press.

Made in the USA
Columbia, SC
18 August 2023

21820501R00033